Holidays and Celebrations
The 100th Day of School

by Brenda Haugen
illustrated by Sheree Boyd

Thanks to our advisers for their expertise, research, and advice:

Alexa Sandmann, Ed.D., Professor of Literacy
The University of Toledo, Toledo, Ohio
Member, National Council for the Social Studies

Susan Kesselring, M.A., Literacy Educator
Rosemount-Apple Valley-Eagan (Minnesota) School District

PICTURE WINDOW BOOKS
MINNEAPOLIS, MINNESOTA

For Loran, MacKenzie, Jordon, and Mr. Bridge

Managing Editor: Bob Temple
Creative Director: Terri Foley
Editor: Sara E. Hoffmann
Editorial Adviser: Andrea Cascardi
Copy Editor: Laurie Kahn
Designer: Melissa Voda
Page production: The Design Lab
The illustrations in this book were rendered digitally.

Picture Window Books

5115 Excelsior Boulevard
Suite 232
Minneapolis, MN 55416
1-877-845-8392
www.picturewindowbooks.com

Printed in the United States of America.

Library of Congress Cataloging-in-Publication Data
Haugen, Brenda.
The 100th day of school / written by Brenda Haugen ; illustrated by Sheree Boyd.
p. cm. — (Holidays and celebrations)
Summary: Briefly discusses the history and customs connected to the celebration of the one hundredth
day of school. Includes bibliographical references (p.   ).
ISBN 1-4048-0196-0 (hardcover)
ISBN 1-4048-0492-7 (softcover)
1. Hundredth Day of School—Juvenile literature. 2. Hundred (The number)—Study and teaching
(Elementary)—Activity programs—Juvenile literature. 3. Education, Elementary—Activity programs—
Juvenile literature. [1. Hundredth Day of School. 2. Hundred (The number) 3. Special days.]
I. Title: Hundredth day of school. II. Boyd, Sheree, ill. III. Title. IV. Holidays and celebrations
(Picture Window Books)
LB3537 .H38 2003
394.26—dc21
                                                                                    2003006100

The kids in Ms. Mix's class
can hardly wait.
Today is a special day.

It's the 100th day of school!

Many schools in the United States and Canada celebrate the 100th day of school.

Scotty and Lisa's class
looked forward to this day.
Ms. Mix planned lots of fun activities.

100th day!

The class started working on projects for the 100th day as soon as the school year began.

Ashley and Alex have been collecting pennies.

Many classes save coins to buy something special for their rooms.

They placed their pennies in a big jar.
Today they will count the coins in the jar.

Ashley and Alex count the pennies.
They put them in piles of 10.

Ten piles make 100 pennies.
One hundred pennies equal one dollar.

On the 100th day
of school, many students
play math games. They learn
about different ways to make
100. Twenty piles of five, 10
piles of 10, and five piles
of 20 each make 100.

In art class, Ms. Cassels gives
each student a cup with 10 plastic beads.
The children make pretty necklaces
with the shiny beads.

Students can refill their paper cups nine times. Each finished necklace has 100 beautiful beads!

Now it is time for science fun.
Jelly beans and a scale—what's this about?

Nicole and Mac count out 100 pieces
of the colorful treat. The class weighs
the jelly beans on the scale.
Then it's time to eat!

Something special is planned in gym class.
It is the 100th-day Olympics!

The students count how many
exercises they can do in 100 seconds.
They do jumping jacks and sit-ups.
They even hop on one foot.

In the classroom, the kids are getting ready to use their imaginations.

The students draw pictures of themselves. The pictures show what the students will look like when they are 100 years old.

Now the special day is done.
They counted and jumped
and ate jelly beans.

What fun everyone had!

You Can Make a 100th-Day Chain

What you need:

scissors

10 sheets of construction paper, each a different color

glue

What you do:

1. Make sure you have an adult to help you.
2. Cut the construction paper in strips big enough to make loops. You will need 10 strips of each color.
3. Take a strip and glue the ends together to make a loop.
4. Take another strip of a different color and place it through the first loop.
5. Glue this second loop's ends together to start your chain.
6. Keep going until all the strips are part of the chain.
7. When you are done, you will have 100 loops in your chain!

Ideas for Celebrating the 100th Day of School

- Some schools use estimation jars on the 100th day of school. Teachers fill jars with small objects, such as paper clips and marbles. The students have to guess which jars have 100 objects in them.

- One class in New York collects 100 cans of food by the 100th day of school. Then the cans are donated to a food shelf.

- Some kindergarten students in Alabama learn about water on the 100th day of school. They get a big tub and fill it with 100 ice cubes. The students try to guess how long it will take for all the ice to melt and become water.

- Many schools have special calendars. They use the calendars to keep track of how many school days they have had.

- At one Wisconsin school, first graders celebrate the 100th day of school by dressing as they would if they were 100 years old. They also talk about events that have happened in the last 100 years.

Words to Know

century—one hundred years

estimation—a guess made by using the information you have

food shelf—a place for people in need to get food. This place also is called a food pantry or a food bank.

imagination—the ability to form pictures in your mind of things that are not present or real

refill—to fill again

100th day!

To Learn More

At the Library

Bauld, Jane Scoggins. **We Need Teachers.** Mankato, Minn.: Pebble Books, 2000.

Cuyler, Margery. **100th Day Worries.** New York: Simon & Schuster Books for Young Readers, 2000.

Harris, Trudy. **100 Days of School.** Brookfield, Conn.: Millbrook Press, 1999.

McMullan, Kate. **Fluffy's 100th Day of School.** New York: Scholastic, 1999.

Wells, Rosemary. **Emily's First 100 Days of School.** New York: Hyperion Books for Children, 2000.

Fact Hound

Fact Hound offers a safe, fun way to find Web sites related to this book. All of the sites on Fact Hound have been researched by our staff.
http://www.facthound.com

1. Visit the Fact Hound home page.
2. Enter a search word related to this book, or type in this special code: 1404801960.
3. Click on the FETCH IT button.

Your trusty Fact Hound will fetch the best sites for you!

Index

beads, 12–13

century, 19

dollar, 11

estimation jars, 23

exercises, 16–17

food shelf, 23

jelly beans, 14–15, 20

Olympics, 16

pennies, 8–11

pictures, 18–19

24